A CLYACK-SHEAF

Hugh MacDiarmid

A Clyack-Sheaf

MACGIBBON & KEE

FIRST PUBLISHED 1969 BY MACGIBBON & KEE LTD
3 UPPER JAMES STREET GOLDEN SQUARE LONDON W1
COPYRIGHT © CHRISTOPHER MURRAY GRIEVE 1969
PRINTED IN GREAT BRITAIN BY
EBENEZER BAYLIS & SON LTD
THE TRINITY PRESS
WORCESTER AND LONDON

SBN 261 62131 9

CONTENTS

FOREWORD

A Clyack-Sheaf, or Maiden, is the last handful of wheat cut down by the reapers on a farm. It is also a name given to the autumnal feast, or Harvest Home.

I have chosen this title since the present collection of poems is a collection excluded from my *Collected Poems* published in America in 1962. The publishers of that volume found it inexpedient to include in it a lot of the poems I had originally sent them for that purpose. The book was consequently mis-titled and unfortunately my Author's Note, intended for the entire collection, was inadvertently retained. It said that the collection contained all the poems written up to that time I had deemed worthy of retention. This, of course, did not apply to what was actually published but to the much bigger collection initially submitted.

The consequence had been that readers all over the world have written to me complaining of the exclusion of items they particularly esteemed. The contents of the present volume rectify that and are a final intaking of my crop of poetry up to that time, with, in addition, a number of poems not previously published at all.

I have called it *a* Clyack-Sheaf—not *The* Clyack-Sheaf—simply because there are other fields of my poet's farm not yet harvested, the present yield being for the most part gleaned from the same acres as my *Collected Poems*.

Biggar, 1969   HUGH MACDIARMID

A CLYACK-SHEAF

Credo

As a poet I'm interested in religious ideas
– Even Scottish ones, even Wee Free ones – as a matter
                                        of fact
Just as an alcoholic can take snake venom
With no worse effects than a warming of the digestive tract.

The Ross-shire Hills

What are the hills of Ross-shire like?
Listen. I'll tell you. Over the snow one day
I went out with my gun. A hare popped up
On a hill-top not very far away.

I shot it at once. It came rolling down
And round it as it came a snowball grew,
Which, when I kicked it open, held not one
But seventeen hares. Believe me or not. It's true.

In Changing Moods (six poems)

I

In these lane voes whaur the airms o' bar land
Lie on the grey waters like shadows oor boat
Seems to haud a' the life that there is – there's nae need
To rin a line oot; there's nae fish to be got
– Yet aye there's a cry, 'I see white in the lum'
And up on the line coontless ferlies come.
Toom tho' the waters may look, useless oor quest,
We find on ilka hook a yield 'yont a' hope
– A scallop, a hoo, a sea-sponge, and syne
A halibut big as a table-top.
Never say die; tho' auld Scotland seems bare
Oot wi' your line; there's prodigies there.

aye – always
ferlies – marvels
Toom – empty

ilka – every
hoo – dog-fish

II

From 'THE WAR WITH ENGLAND'

I was better with the sounds of the sea
    than with the voices of men
And in desolate and desert places
    found myself again.
For the whole of the world came from there
And he who returns to the source
May gauge the worth of the outcome
And approve and perhaps reinforce
Or disapprove and perhaps change its course.

Now I deal with the hills at their roots
    and the streams at their springs
And am for the land I love
    as he who brings
His bride home, and they know each other
Not as erst, like their friends, they have done
But carnally, causally, knowing that only
By life nigh undone can life be begun
    and accept and are one.

III

A great inheritance! The tale is scarce begun.
The outer and the inner Hebrides,
The Dungeon amid the dark Merricks,
Cairnamuir and the Cruives of Cree,
Lone St. Mary's silent lake,
Broomy Bemersyde, Flodden Field,
Lincluden, Ellisland, Penpont,
Drumlanrig, Durisdeer, Enterkin Pass,
The Bullers of Buchan, the Laich of Moray,
The enchanted land of Drumalbain,
Kintyre, Crinan, Lorne, Inverness, Scone,
Dunfermline, Edinburgh, Perth, Stirling
– The successive stages of the Scottish Kingdom;
I see them all, an innumerable host,
As Mistral saw the 'lou regard pacifi de mis Aupiho bluio',
'L'immense Crau, la Crau peirouso . . .
La mudo Crau, la Crau deserto . . .'
Singing not of particular deeds and persons
But of a whole land and a whole people,
And, beginning with his native region,
Ended by embracing all nations
In one *amphictyoneia* – a vision in *parvo*
Of the labours of all mankind.
Every form of work appears,
Be it for a second only,
In *Mireio*. Up and down the Rhône
Pass all aspects of humanity,
Pope and Emperor, harlot and convict,
And the manifold elements are grouped together
In one final hubbub
At the fair of Beaucaire.
So I hold all Scotland
In my vision now
– A Falkirk Tryst of endless comprehension and love.

In the wonderful diversity and innumerable
Sharp transitions of the Scottish scene,
The source of our Scottish antisyzygy,
Grundvorstellung des mannigfaltigsten Umschlags,
I who used to deplore the incredible shallowness
Of all but all of my fellow-countrymen,
So out of keeping with the Scottish mountains
Far more of them surely should have resembled,
Each with a world in himself,
Each full of darkness like a mountain,
Each deep in his humbleness
Without fear of abasing himself
And therefore pious,
People full of remoteness, uncertainty, and hope,
People who were still evolving,
Suddenly (my master Shestov's *suddenly*!)
See now the reconciliation of all opposites,
Das Offene, das Ganze, das Sein, der Weltinnenraum
And understand how '. . . der reine Widerspruch
                                des kosmischen Seins
– Die Tatsache, dass pas, was dem Menschen
                                nur im Umschlag
Im kosmischen immer schonzusammen ist.'

IV

To hell wi' happiness!
I sing the terrifyin' discipline
O' the free mind that gars a man
Make his joys kill his joys,
The weakest by the strongest,
The temporal by the fundamental
(Or hope o' the fundamental)
And prolong wi'in himself
Threids o' thocht sae fragile
It needs the help and continuance
O' a' his vital power
To haud them frae brakin'
As he pou's them owre the gulfs.
Oor humanity canna follow us
To lichts sae faur removed.
A man ceases to be himsel'
Under sicna constraint.
Will he find life or daith
At the end of his will,
At thocht's deepest depth,
Or some frightfu' sensation o' seein'
Nocht but the ghastly glimmer
O' his ain puir maitter?
     What does it maitter?
     It's the only road.
The beaten track is *beaten* frae the stert.

Man's the reality that mak's
A'thing possible, even himsel'!
Energy's his miracle,
But hoo little he's dune wi't yet,
Denyin't at ilka turn.
Ilka change has Eternity's mandate.
But hoo little we've changed since Adam!

gars – makes ilka – every wi't – with it

16

V

Half a millennium ago in adamantine verse
Proudly utilising a wealth of historical truth
George Buchanan celebrated in the Scottish people
A cat-like vitality, through many centuries forsooth,
Like that amazing vigour, vitality, strength,
Of the common people of Spain, which saw unexhausted
Romans, Visigoths, Moors, Napoleon
– That 'Improvisación creadora ibérica',
The indefinable quality which astounded
                Napoleon and Wellington.

It is gone, forever, incredibly, gone.
Fain would I cry again today
'My faith is in the Commons of Scotland',
But alas! it is gone, it is a' wede away.
Scotland is in the last stages of the fell disease
ἀβουλα; and in its glens there is only peace . . . peace?

The peace indeed that passeth understanding!
For Scotland – Scotland! – has thrown her hand in!
And Alba[1] produces a wretched alibi
At the bar of human history.
The people crawl about – decaying things.
Their clothes like damp mould on trees, their faces green.
Beyond all doctoring – ghosts, we gaze at each other
As though the River of Oblivion ran between;
Vitality, mentality, spirituality, sociality,
All sucked away . . .

[1] Alba (i.e. Scotland), pronounced Alaba

VI

When I see a possible poem, I work
With the utmost economy of effort.
The old scarred Visalia Kak is stripped
To fundamentals – the skirts trimmed down
Till they barely cover the tree – the stirrups
Cut off close to the rosettes. No stirrup fenders,
And the doubled stirrup straps wrapped
With rawhide to keep the stirrups in position.
A lass-rope and hackamore
Complete my equipment
– And you can bet your boots I'm going to take
A good whirl at breaking it!
And ever and again it shall be with me
As when on the night called *lailat ul mi'raj*
Muhammad ascended to Heaven from Jerusalem
On the fabulous mule named Burak.

In Berwickshire Again

This is the full, the immarcesible flower
I divined long ago in the bud
When I first trod the rough track that runs
Along the Allt na Bogair
Up to the shoulder of Meall a Bhuic,
And turning found myself looking
Over the blue waters of Loch Rannoch
To the whole snow-capped range
Of the Grampians and Cairngorms
– One of the most stupendous views
In all Scotland, and only to be seen
By the airman, rider, or walker,
Being far beyond the reach
Of car or tram

And there as I found myself,
Topping the glen, in the presence
Of scores of stags almost indistinguishable
From the moorland on which they fed,
And, overhead, black specks in the sky,
Saw wheeling, falling,
Circling at tremendous heights,
The golden eagles, safe
In their empyrean liberty,
And knew squadrons of bomber planes
Would never fly there instead,
I cried: Here is the real Scotland.
The Scotland of the leaping salmon,
The soaring eagle, the unstalked stag,
And the leaping mountain hare.
Here, above the tree-line, where the track
Is the bed of an amethystine burn
In a bare world of shining quartz and purple heather

Is the Scotland that is one of the sights of the earth
And once seen can never be forgotten.

This, not Edinburgh and Glasgow, which are rubbish,
The Scotland of the loathsome beasties climbing the wall
And the rats hunting in the corners
Which is next to impossible to believe
Coexists with this, and men value – *Men?*
And now as I look at the whole of Scotland
I feel as though I had Furmanov[1] with me
And am discussing it all with him
In an atmosphere very similar
To that crystal-like, serious, and thrilling attention
Which characterised the creation of *Chapayev*,
Furmanov, with that special quality he had
Of being able to see himself objectively,
To weigh himself in the scales of the Communist Cause,
As I here my devotion to Scotland
In the balance of the whole world's purpose.

I have come to this height as of old
In Berwickshire I thridded the 'Pass of Peaths',
'So steepe be these banks on either syde
And so depe to the bottom
That who goeth straight downe
Shall be in danger of tumbling
And the comer-up so sure
Of puffyng and payne; for remedy whereof
The travellers that way have used to pass it
By paths and footways leading slopewise';
And fortified against the English at the East Lothian end
By Scottish trenches, 'rather hindering than letting'.
It was a difficult passage to put into prose

[1] D. A. Furmanov, first Secretary of the Moscow Association of Proletarian Writers,
and, in reality, the creator of this fighting organisation, which gathered under its wing
the overwhelming majority of the growing proletarian cadres of Soviet literature.

For an invader sworn not to step one foot
Out of his predetermined course.
But the part of Scotland brimful of life at the full
Into which it gave was the only part
Of Scotland in the past that was ever fulfilled
Like the whole of Scotland in my vision now.

Unlike any other part of Scotland
And more unlike, needless to say, any region of England;
No lush hedgerows, no flowery lanes,
No picturesque unkempt orchards, no crooked lines;
A garden of twenty or thirty acre fields
Geometrically laid out and divided
By well-built walls or low-clipped thorn fences
Upon either side of which no foot of space
Was given to the unprofitable or picturesque in nature.

This is the cream of the country – probably
The cream of the earth, the famous Dunbar red lands.
These red loams combine a maximum of fertility
With friable easy-working qualities of unequalled perfection.
Potatoes, a level sea of lusty shaws and flowery tops
From fence to fence in summer-time,
Then wheat, going to eight quarters an acre,
And then the swedes and turnips
Flickering strong and lusty
In the wind over the large fields
And much fitter to hold birds
Than many a southern rootfield in early September.

No waste ground here – nor open ditches,
Nor rambling fences, nor tousely corners,
Nor ragged headlands, nor hedgerow timber
To draw the land and obstruct the sunshine!
The crop pushes stiff and level
Up to the stone wall or trim thorn hedge

Which, in the growing and maturing season,
Subside – as all over Scotland
In my vision now –
Into thin faint lines hardly discernible
Amid the lush abundance.
And with me men like Henderson of Chirnside
– Admirable people, so fashioned that their native district
Provides an inexhaustible mine
Of affectionate interest and study of its people,
Its customs, antiquities, scenery,
Birds, beasts, flowers.
Every countryside has happily a few
Who have eyes to see and ears to hear
In this sense, and ask for nothing better,
And what could be better, than to use and enjoy
These too-rare faculties and this happy temperament
Upon the soil that bred them and for love of it.

Now I remember in particular an inn near Coldingham.
Mine host was a man after my own heart,
A veteran of character and long memory,
A sportsman, a farmer, and, among other things,
A master-hand at a 'crack',
And when a Scotsman shines in this,
And he very often does, he is hard to beat.

So far as I have known both upon their native heath
Along the Border, he is more efficient in this particular
Than his ancient enemy, the Northumbrian.
His Doric is richer and even racier; he has also
The undoubted advantage of his Rs in emphasis,
When, that is to say,
There is life and character behind them.
And men with a twinkling eye have always seemed to me
More abundant upon the left than upon the right bank
                              of Tweed,

– Around the Lammermoors than along the Cheviots –
Dour as is the average hind
In the low country of either.

Now I see all my land and my people
As I saw Berwickshire and East Lothian then,
With every potentiality completely realized,
Brimming with prosperity and no waste anywhere,
And note once more as I cast my eyes this way and that
How the healthy well-fed flickering turnip breadths
Are more vivid in their green between the woods,
And even that homely article, the potato,
When clustering over a thirty-acre field
With the slanting sun upon it
Contributes a characteristic note.
And how every one of the streams of the Merse
Brings the spirit of the mountains and the wild
Into the rich low ground, and retains the buoyancy
Of its clear amber waters until its voice
Is ultimately silenced in the wide swish of the Tweed.
With fine disregard for the well-ordered landscape,
Its pride of timber and its pride of crop,
See how the impetuous Whiteadder churns
In the deep twisting valley its chafing waters
Have cut in the course of ages
Through the sandstone! Narrow breadths of green meadow
Serve to set off the glitter of its rapid currents
And take no great injury from its floods.
Chafing always upon a rocky bed
The river gathers round it
All that fine tangle of foliage
You see only upon impetuous streams
And so to the Berwickshire Bounds, these few thousand acres
Of cornland windswept from the North Sea
– Surely 'but scant counterpoise
For sunny Aquitaine and Guienne,

Opulent Bordeaux and the Pas de Calais,
All lost to the Crown of England
In the Hundred Years' War
  – Part of the price
    Paid for the lesson
    That Scotsmen may never be coerced.

And now I am where, upon Hardens Hill,
After trailing between fine avenues of beech and ash,
And mounting higher into wind-swept pine woods,
The road sweeps out at last
Into the glorious heaths of Lammermoor.
The drubbing wings and vocal plaints
Of restless peewits close overhead,
The song of rejoicing larks
In the air far above them,
And the call of distant curlews
Mingle with the fain bleat of sheep.
These edges of great moorlands, which open wide
Upon the one hand into sweeps of solitude,
And on the other over vast distances
Where rural life is thickly humming,
Are seats for the gods indeed!
And I am indeed of the Duine Sidhe[1] today
The heather is just touching with its first faint flush
The folding hills that heave away
Towards a far horizon that looks down
Upon East Lothian. Below,
The Merse glimmers far and wide
With its red fields, its yellowing cornlands and mantling woods,
Its glint of village church spire or country seat,
Beyond the line of Tweed spread the fainter
But yet clear-cut hills and valleys of Northumberland.
I can follow up the windings of the Till
From Flodden and Ford Castle to Wooler,

[1] Gods of the Earth.

And from Wooler to the woody spur
Beneath which the wild white cattle
Of Chillingham have their immemorial range.
The Cheviots roll their billowy crests
From the 'Mickle Cheevit'
Looming large and near upon the Border line
To fade remotely into the more rugged heights
That embosom Rothbury
And the upper waters of the Coquet.
And in fancy I drink once again
– A final toast to Scotland fulfilled,
Every promise redeemed –
With one of the many hundreds of splendid men
With whom I have so drunk in days gone by.
Not drinking whisky and soda
As an Englishman does, which is very dull,
But with all the splendid old ritual,
The urn, the rummers, the smaller glasses,
The silver ladles, and the main essentials.
The whisky toddy is mixed in a rummer,
A round-bottomed tumbler on a stem,
And transferred at intervals with a silver ladle
Into an accompanying wine-glass
By way of cooling it
Sufficiently for consumption.

Time which has brought such prodigious changes
In the world below and in the world at large
Has here at least stood absolutely still.
The same old cry of curlews and wail of peewits,
Whistling of golden plover, call of anxious grouse,
Plash of waters, and bleat of far-scattered sheep
Still sounds the same unchanging music of the wild,
Black peat-hags, glistening mosses of emerald green,
Tawny moor-grasses flecked white with the wild
                              cotton-flower,

Scaurs of red sandstone, and vivid patches
Of sheep-nibbled turf,
All add their note.

This is the full, the immarcesible flower,
Scotland, known like the music of a moorland stream,
To which poets and musicians pay conventional tribute,
But which few can approach with an understanding
Of what it means to an old fisherman
Who knows its infinite varieties of chord and melody
With an intimacy of a thousand day-long recitations.

Known, as often old gardeners and farm-hands
Understand the personality, as it were,
Of individual fields and gardens
To which they have ministered since boyhood
And their fathers perhaps before them.
For the constitution of a piece of land
Is more than skin-deep and draws
Some of its peculiar characteristics
From geological depths.
Pedology may tell us *why* a soil
Behaves as it does,
But only a rustic knows exactly *when*,
And, familiar with a tract of land, can often say
Without going to it
When the day has come to find it
In a humour to respond
To the caress of a harrow
Or when it will be found
As obdurate as iron.
But this is a kind of knowledge
Scotland has lost almost altogether,
Blighted in the shadow of great institutions
Of learning designed
For the depotentization of free intelligence,

The Fascist barracks of our universities,
The murder machine of our whole educational system.
And far gone towards that Nazism
Which is at bottom
A revolution of black-coated workers,
Multiplied in number by social conditions,
Striving for jobs they feel suitable
To their training and dignity;
Scotland drowned under a percentage of clerks
That is rising by leaps and bounds!
And it's O for the Berwickshire bondagers[1]
And the country folk and fisher folk of old,
And many a great day I had with them
Fifty years ago now!
– *Ah! quam dulce est meminisse!*
– We have fallen upon lean days.
Would Burns have sparkled upon small ale
And how would the Ettrick Shepherd
Who took his whisky in a jug
Fare in a time like this?

All the clerks in Scotland are not worth one glimpse
Of an East Lothian bailiff I knew then
With a voice that could carry nearly all over
The six hundred acres of his farm
And a whistle that would carry
Even further than his voice
And not a tree or a bush in the whole place
To break the force of either
(Just as there is no higher ground between us here
And the Ural Mountains in the East!)
When he appeared at the gate of a thirty-acre field
The subdued cackle of the bondagers ceased abruptly
And twenty poke bonnets, bent over their Dutch hoes,

---

[1] Women field workers.

Pushed with renewed zeal along the wheat drills,
And the ploughman halting for a moment on the headrigg
Started and swung his pair of horses round
And geehawed away for his life
When he heard that voice two fields away.
Across the heavy-laden grainfields;
Over the great broad rectangles of potato land,
Thigh deep in their dark green covering of shaws:
Beyond the flickering blue-green tops of the thickly-clustering swedes,
Or the paler pastures, where heavy Border Leicesters,
Or their crosses are lazily grazing the rye grass and clover ley
And tramping it hard for the autumn ploughing,
And between the woods the indeterminate line of the shore
And the gleam of the sea beyond,
Fading into the far-spreading woods of Tynninghame
. . . The sudden unfolding of the greatest of agricultural countries,
Girt about with wide waters and shadowy mountains.

If a vista of plain and mountain appeals solely
To his artistic sense, and man is obviously incapable
Of reading any deeper into it or of responding
To any other appeal, there is nothing more to be said.
No undervaluing of the elevating influence of nature,
Unilluminated by anything but its own form and colouring,
On the senses is intended here; yet this is not
To 'feel' a country, but only its physical surface,
Which might be occupied by negroes
Without the least disturbance of the emotions engaged.
But the great thing is to be able to drop at once
Into terms of intimacy with the local *genii*
Till, whether it be the Tees, the Greta, the Trossachs, or the
                                        Welsh Border,
All the rivers for you sound their tales, the woods shake out
                                        their secrets.

In Memoriam Garcia Lorca

Lorca! 'Pensive, merry, and dear to the people
As a guitar, simple-hearted and responsive as a child
– His whole life was helpful and inspiring to others
And he earned his people's deep and lasting affection.'[1]
Lorca's love of his people, clear in his writings,
Met with a passionate response. His songs and ballads
Were quickly caught up all over revolutionary Spain.
The Fascist henchmen could never forgive
His popularity and devotion to the people.
They shot him and made a bonfire of his books
On Carmen Square in Granada.
'Fear not! This debt we shall repay!'[2]
Lorca's poetry, however, can never be silenced.
It will continue to blow as free as the wind
Over the wide spaces of heroic Spain.
Lorca, dead, lives forever.

The poet has been turned into earth and silence,
Yet every day he dies and resuscitates in the heart of Spain,
In the heart of the world, because today the world
Bleeds and throbs together with the people of Spain
– Angel Lazaro is right when he cries:
'How was it that the murderers' bullets did not stop
Before that brow
Below which the angels of verse
Sang a matchless music?
I think of that head struck to the ground
The black lock fallen as though it wanted to go
With the last stertor
To the thread of recondite water

[1] From Pablo Neruda's tribute to Lorca.
[2] From lines addressed to Lorca by Luis de Tapia.

Of his Andalusia.
I think of Lorca dead – he who stood upright
In the middle of life
Like a young bull in the middle of the fields.
I think of the last terror of his pupils,
Those pupils that had known how to see
Unique colours and foreshortenings of wonder,
And thinking of that
I cannot utter any word but this:
Murderers! Murderers!

To Those of my Old School
who fell in the Second World War

One loves the temporal, some unique manifestation,
Something irreplaceable that dies.

But one is loyal to an ideal limit
Involved in all specific objects of love
And in all co-operating wills.

Shall the lonely griefs and joys of men
Forever remain a pluralistic universe?
Need they, if thought and will are bent in common interest
In making this universe one?

All these things are clearer to me today than ever;
The ineluctable individuation of personality,
The importance of indefinables in life,
The moral urgency of definition
If we are to make secure for Eternity
The treasures of the moment,
– As you, comrades of my old school,
Have helped to add
One of the sublimest sagas of human courage
To the whole history of Mankind!
Shown again the individual is the only foundation
On which any social order may safely build;
That David can still stand up against Goliath,
That the individual can still
Be the master of his fate, the captain of his soul;
That man is still the potential creator
Rather than the victim of his creations;
A creature of free will and untold possibilities,
Not the slave of environment;
His capabilities limited not so much
By heredity or poverty as by his own vision of himself.

I thank you – and the whole world has cause to thank you –
For the rediscovery of man and the powers
Of which he is capable when his mind has been freed
From fallacies about himself.
I thank you, comrades of my old school,
For this timely and invaluable reassurance
– For vouchsafing us so wonderful a spectable
Of the movement of individual will
Towards a common beckoning Good,
Always distant, yet always implicit
In love and understanding,
And the only alternative to callousness and despair;
And for all the glimpses you have given us
Of the incredible beauty
Of those who give themselves while they are yet young
Selflessly to a noble cause.

Symbol of human freedom forever,
You endured more
Than any other citizen army in history,
Even that which, in June 1778
Marched on the heels of the retreating British
With William Billings, 'blind and slovenly'
But full of fire, setting the key for the song:
'Let tyrants shake their iron rods
And Slavery clank her galling chains;
We wear them not . . .'

Neither legends nor lies are needed,
The truth is enough. It should stiffen the spines
Of all who fear for human liberty. You, comrades,
Who froze and starved and rotted in this War,
Were not superhuman; you merely preferred
Suffering and death
Rather than bend your knees
To persons and principles you rightly despised.

Wherefore, in every man and woman of you on the Allied side,
I see that unconscious processes may be intelligent and aspiring,
Generating images and intuitions of moral import,
Solutions of conflict, desirable avenues of advance.
In presenting you thus I function as a priest
But outside all systems of theology.
I see your War as an exciting drama
In which you are all Platonic forms and archetypes;
Vast images that illumine, guide, and make significant
The most trivial occurrences.

Behind all this is an idea,
Suggested by indirection,
Of the human soul, its creative evolution,
Its enlightenment, its fulfilment in relationship
Not with some imaginary deity
But with the boundless potentialities
Of other creative individuals;
And your story is thus a revealing mirror
That will instigate
A Resurrection from the Dead!
You will be remembered when your foes are forgotten,
On the one side – the People,
On the other – the vain trifles and vicious wealth
Of a worthless few. Chartres versus Versailles!
Versailles! symbol of the 'model kingship
In our civilisation' – vast, ornate,
Magnificent, overpowering,
Wholly unconnected with the real life of the nation,
Sterile always,
As it is silent and empty now,
Trivial, ephemeral, dead!
Nobody remembers
What kings reigned in France
When the people of Beauce were building their cathedral;
And their days like all life

Knew poverty
And ignorance and oppression and suffering,
But the living force and beauty
In the minds and souls of many men
Created in their work a vital glory.

So, today, hope lies
In the free and many-sided spirit of humanity
Against any one-man Domination.
Beyond the meaningless and dead splendours of Versailles
The glowing beauty of Chartres
Speaks imperishably through the ages,
And even so will the future see you,
Little group of comrades from my old school,
Who went out
Against the Powers and Principalities of Darkness.

Hail and farewell, my friends!
At the moment it seems
As though the pressure of a loving hand had gone,
The touch
Under which my close-pressed fingers seemed to thrill
And the skin divide up into little zones
Of heat and cold whose position continually changed
So that the whole of my hand, held in that clasp,
Was in a state of internal movement.
My eyes – that were full of pride,
My hands – that were full of love,
Are empty again – for a while,
For a little while!

The International Brigade

Honour forever to the International Brigade!
They are a song in the blood of all true men.

The men of each nation showed qualities of their own.
The Swiss formidable for their dour obstinacy
And their concentrated, fretful impatience when not attacking;
The Poles kind-hearted, romantic, dashing, and absolutely fearless;
The English treat the war as a kind of job that has to be done
And they do it well (the pacifists from the English Universities
Make excellent machine-gunners). The Bulgarians
Have a preference for the hand-grenade. They resemble
The Spanish 'dynamiters' who storm machine-gun positions
With hand-made grenades. The French have the greatest number
Of deserters because it is easier for them
Than for any others both to come and go.
The French who remain are men of prodigious valour
And impetuosity. The Americans are an élite
By reason of their sober courage
And their simple keen intelligence.
The Germans are the best that Germany can give
(and that is saying much) many of them
Hardened by persecution and with much to avenge.

But if there had been a vote in the column
The Italians would have been shown as the favourites;
They combined a passionate chivalry and devotion
With supreme courage, resourcefulness, and discipline.
There can be no doubt at all that the Italian
Is a first-rate soldier when he is fighting
                              For a cause he has at heart.

The battle of Guadalajara brought face to face

Anti-Fascist Italians fighting
For an ideal to which they had dedicated their lives,
And Italians sent to Spain
To fight in a cause completely unknown to them.
Many of the latter had been deliberately tricked:
Signed on to be sent to Ethiopia
Where there would be work for them
And a livelihood for their families.
No interest of their country was at stake in Spain.
They had no reason to fight against the Spanish people,
Nor to shed their blood
For Spanish generals, bishops, and big landowners.
The alleged menace of Communism
Left them indifferent. What had they to lose
If Communism triumphed in Spain?
Or even in Italy? Wealth? They had none.
Liberty? They had none. To crown all
They found themselves fighting against Italians
Whose banner bore the name of Garibaldi
No wonder they listened to their fellow-countrymen
And refused to fight in a cause
Which could never be theirs.

No man worth calling a man can deny
The wonder and glory of the International Brigade.
They will live in history forever.
All the secrecy, sordidness, scheming and lying of the
                                        Non-Interventionists
Was the fault of stuffy fools who are afraid of liberty.
                        The wide imaginative vision
Which touches the soul with the golden light of pity
Is hopelessly absent from every word they say.

How could they possibly understand such men?
Ideals of duty and sacrifice, firmly grasped,
                        And faithfully followed,

Led them to the starry heights where life
Becomes a divine adventure, and death
                            But an interlude leading
                            To yet more glorious achievement.

The soul of man became in them a dominant thing,
Its indestructibility in a world falling in ruins
Among scenes of indescribable horror
A thing to be held on to passionately.

They rang true. Is there more than one man
In a hundred thousand anywhere else
Of whom it is possible to say that
Courage and honesty
Are the foundations of his nature?

It is very rarely that a man loves
And when he does it is nearly always fatal.

The fire of life woke and burnt in these men
With that clear and passionate flame
That can only burn in those whose hearts are clean.
We were transported into the flaming heart of the world;
We stood in a place to which all roads came;
In a light which made all riddles clear.

Love and Pain, Terror and Ecstasy,
Strife and Fulfilment, Blasphemy and Prayer
                          Were one anothers' shadows,
Meeting and fading in a single radiance
                          That was not light nor heat,
But a movement, a flowing, that carried us along
And yet left us steadier,
                          More certain than we ever were before.

Plaster Madonna

In the baptistry of a village Church in the Pyrenées
An Anarchist militiaman said to me
'This damned junk' – and he pointed
To the charred and tumbled mummery before the church –
'Is still *alive* in the minds of many of our people.
Once, perhaps, it comforted them.
Now it is just a lingering and shadowy fear.'
He told me a legend from his own town, Arenys de Mar.
The people of Arenys commissioned a statue of the Virgin
From a famous image maker of Palma de Majorca.
A tremendous storm arose soon after
The statue-bearing ship had left Palma Bay,
And not all the prayers and entreaties of the crew
Could secure divine help against the storm.
Suddenly one of the seamen understood
What had happened – and rushing to the box
In which the image was packed, he turned it over,
Whereupon the storm went down.
The Virgin had been laid face downward
And to express her displeasure
Had raised the storm.
How charming, you say, a fine, dramatic, mediaeval legend!
No such thing. In Arenys the old women will tell you
The date of that storm. It was 1861.
Do you begin to see the truth in the Anarchist's statement –
That minds whose imaginations are controlled
By a culture of this type
Can never hope to live happily
In a world that has placed
New techniques and new responsibilities
                    In people's hands? Gad, sir,
That seaman's 'understanding' of the trouble
Is precisely all the 'understanding'
Of the Right ever amounts to.

For Daniel Cohn-Bendit

(On the occasion of his candidature in Glasgow
University Rectorial Election, 1968[1])

No man or group of men has any right
To force another man or other groups of men
To do anything he or they do not wish to do.
There is no right to govern without
The consent of the governed. Consent is not only
Important in itself, and as a nidus for freedom
And its attendant spontaneity, (clearly valuable
As the opposed sense of frustration is detrimental)
                    But the sole
Basis of political obligation. There is nothing
Supplemental to or coequal with consent itself
And even if we had not the lessons of all history
– The endless evidence of 'man's inhumanity to man'
And overwhelming proof that all power debases
And that no man is good enough to have it
Or can exercise it without doing far more harm than good –
The contention is utterly indefensible – sheer humbug! mortmain!
That 'so long as the exercise of certain powers is good in itself
Or a means to the good . . . these powers are right
Whether or not anyone is of the opinion that they are,'
The time-dishonoured formula that attempts to conceal or excuse
All the hellish wrong of human history,
The fraud and loss inherent in all Government,
That age-long monstrous distortion of the faculties of man
It is the great historical task of the working-class
To eliminate today, no matter at what cost,
That human life, no longer wrenched hideously awry,
May spring up at last in its proper form.

[1] The author was one of Cohn-Bendit's sponsors on this occasion.

Goodbye Twilight

Back to the great music, Scottish Gaels. Too long
You have wallowed as in the music of Delius.
Make a heroic effort now to swing yourselves round
To the opposite pole – the genius of Sibelius.
(Out of the West Highlands and Islands of Scotland now
What a symphony should come, more ghastly and appalling
That Sibelius's gaunt El-Greco-emaciated ecstatic Fourth!
Far beyond *Squinting Peter's Flame of Wrath*
Or *Too long in This Condition*[1]
But like the great jigs, whirling electrons of musical energy,
Like *The Shaggy Grey Buck* or *The Baldooser*,
Fantastic, incredible, all but impossible to human fingers.

It is impossible perhaps to imagine two men
More utterly unlike in temperament than these.
Sibelius lacks wholly the rather morbid preoccupation
With what is vaguely termed 'Nature' Delius possesses,
An obsession that does not allow of any very clear
Spiritual vision or insight into the true inwardness of the thing
That is the obsession. Delius looks upon 'Nature' and
                                        promptly becomes
Doped, drugged, besotted – my countrymen, even as you.

Sibelius, on the other hand, keeps all his very fine
Acute Northern wits – not a commodity to be found
Growing on blackberry bushes here in the North, you know –
Very well on the alert; he knows
That that aspect of the matter is an aspect only,
That there's much more to it than only that,
And the magic of his Finland is in his very nerves and bones
As the magic of our Scotland should be in ours.

[1] Titles of two of the great *piobaireachd*.

If and when he does indulge in a specific piece
Of 'nature' writing, as in the *Oceanides*, one has the feeling
That in those parts at least it is felt and he too fells
That the outward aspect of the thing vaguely called 'nature'
Is itself a magical manifestation as much as
Any transportation, materialisation, or like phenomenon might be.

Delius merely exclaims, with a catch of his breath,
'Oh, how lovely! – and how sad it must all come to an end!'
And promptly dissolves into tears. Sibelius
Does not think or feel it sad at all.
Anyhow, what about the magician? The contrast in outlook
and temper
Makes itself vividly felt in a prolonged listening
To the two. A long spell of Delius
Is enervating and relaxing like a muggy winter day in London,
While Sibelius charges his hearer with nervous energy
Almost as if he had performed some operations of *Prana*
with him.
Back to the great music, you fools – to the classical Gaelic
temper!
Out of the Celtic Twilight and into the Gaelic sun!

In portions of his writings Franz Kafka deals
With the material of his own obsessions,
The sub-conscious mechanisms are never allowed
To throw up fantasy uncriticised, but continually
Put through a checking process . . . whereas you
With the best intentions in the world get nowhere
Because your sub-conscious nature, which, apparently
You know nothing about, is manipulating you from the start.

Out from your melancholy moping, your impotence, Gaels,
(You stir the heart, you think? . . . but surely
One of the heart's main functions is to supply the brain!)

Back into the real world again – the world once of *The*
                                        Barren Rocks of Aden,
The 79th Farewell to Gibraltar, Kantara to El-Arish,
And, now, the world of Barke's *Scottish Ambulance Unit in*
                                        Spain
– For the true spirit is still living here and there, and perhaps
The day is not far distant when the Scottish people
Will enter into this heritage, and in so doing
Enrich the heritage of all mankind again.

When the Birds Come Back to Rhiannon

Once more a man cried
(Passionately identifying himself
With the whole of Scotland
From top to bottom,
Surveying entire Scotland with his mind's eye
– To hear his phrases was like watching a fog rise;
We saw great tracts of country, roadless, unvisited,
Rare flowers and birds in inaccessible places,
Rocky formations, currents, soils,
Weather conditions, caves, legends, antiquities.
He sang the whole song of Scotland
With a marvellous gift for seizing the mood of Nature,
A profound animistic understanding,
A lyrical genius giving a sense of revelation,
Conjuring up an open country, ploughed all over,
Surging like the sea, its horizons sleeping under a misty haze.
Its landscapes were filled with life
– Alive as these old woodcuts in which we see
Men, animals, and birds all going about their business,
Each completely in character,
As if they had just stepped out of the Ark.
He painted not outside time and space,
But rather in a time and space
Enlarged by the force of emotion
– A comprehensive poetic grasp of appearance)
Quoting from the breastplate of St. Patrick:

> 'I bind to myself today
> The power of Heaven,
> The light of the sun,
> The whiteness of snow,
> The force of fire,
> The flashing of lightning,
> The velocity of wind,

The depth of the sea,
The stability of the earth,
The hardness of rocks.'

His indeed was the eloquence
Elusive at shape-shifting as the Mor-rigu,
A power of the word in the blood,
By virtue of which as Plato says,
He conformed his soul
To the motion of the heavenly bodies.
He had been given to drink of Conndla's Well,
Where grew the hazels of wisdom and inspiration.
(Had his quest been for wisdom only he had
Like Sinann been overcome by its waters
And verily tasted of death!)
Pure of heart and aright with nature
And having read the runes and rubrics of the spirit,
Cliadna Fairhead, of the race of Gods,
Had bestowed on him the Cuach of emerald
Which translates water into luscious wine,
Along with the three duo-coloured birds
Of infinite comfort and beguilement,
He brought the notes from the deeps of time
And the tale from the heart of the man who made it,
Knew the colour of Fingal's hair, and saw
The moonlight on the hoods of the Druids.
He had visited the Golden Tree
Which reaches the clouds for height.
And the words being in his heart for a song
And the beat on his pulse for rhythm,
As Caoilte had it in his foot for running,
He got the notes for the tune
In the music of the branches which,
Says the Filidh with the artful thought,
Guards the eloquence and judgement
Of the children of Gaeldom.

The rede is for the wary.
Druidical tenets demanded and received
Purity of thought and material chastity.
And out of the wonderful artistry
Of the illuminated manuscripts of Celtic art
And the age-laden Sagas
He had seen emerge, and understood,
Anaglyphs of ethnic fusions
– A struggling of the spirit for permanent possession,
And by the antennae of this provective spirit
Vanishing epos reappeared
And for this and many such cognate epos
He had rediscovered the alumni of Dagda;
Amairgen the just; Medb of the Sithe;
Merlin or Merwyden; Oengus Mac ind Oc,
The wisest and most cunning of Tuath de Danann;
Ossian in Tir-nan-Og;
The Fianns in their last convulsions;
Defending the royal harp of Tara;
And well he knew the word-magic of the bard, MacCoise,
Who, for the purposes of his art,
Could invoke and receive from Elathan (Skill)
The panegyrics of MacLonam;
The tales of Leech Liathmhuim;
The proverbs of Fitheal;
The eloquence of Fearceartais;
The intellect of the bardess Etain;
The brilliance of Nera,
And the clear truths of Mor-Mumhau.
Having traced and found the footmarks
Of Gael and Cymric from the shadows of the Himalayas,
The mystic regions of Irak,
Across the trails of continents
To the Isle of Saints and to Barra,
He knew from his childhood days
The world must yet seek

Further spiritual creations
From the awakened Celt
Ere the last of the race passed
To join his deathless kin in Tir-nan-Og.
And discovered in himself 'the word of knowledge'
With which Amairgen 'fashioned fire in the head'
And set himself to master 'the marvel of honey verse
With lines of long alliterative words
And sweet compacted syllables, and feet
Increasing upon feet' – and to learn
Enchantments such as Aefi played
On the De Danann children.

And in due time
He raised the wizard horn of the Fingalian heroes
And the voice of bards was tuned in his song.
His was the 'beguiling song of far-off voices',
The spirit-tongued Echo of Prometheus Unbound,
Showing the Coolins of Skye,
The Scurr of Eigg, and the Bens of Jura
As the Crom-Sleuchd of the bard's confessional,
– The beacon-heads from which the shades of the Druids
Transmit the secrets of their Pherylt
To those selected of our race
Who inherit the gift of song.
No longer then need Cathmor transmit
His despairing monody from the Hall of the Winds.
The choristers in the Palace of Enchantment are again
astir.

Magnetic clouds raise high the Silver Shield
That it may re-echo the song of joy.
An Deo-Greine, Fionn's banner, cracks crisply all over
the world.

The birds have come back to Rhiannon,
The rainbow of promise hangs resplendent over Gaeldom
today,

The mysterious prophecies of Merlin
Are being fulfilled in our generation
Now that the solemn but chivalrous practices
Of the Celtic peoples of history are applied
In the light of modern knowledge
To soften international and individual asperities,
Humanity, with a 'pulse like a cannon'
Will co-ordinate in faith and charity
And swing its aspirations forward
Towards peace and goodwill to men.

An English War Poet[1]

In another respect the Spanish War
– Fought on the Republican side
Not by doped conscripts, foreign mercenaries, professional
                                        soldiers,
And Moors and worse than Moors,
But by men who passionately believed
In the cause for which they fought –
Has stamped all the men I know
As members of the International Brigade
With a different bearing together
Than even the best, the most anti-militarist, gained
Of those who fought against Germany in the first Great War.
There in a man like Siegfried Sassoon, for example,
Despite the undeniable honesty, the little literary gift,
What is *Sherston's Progress* but an exposure
Of the eternal Englishman
Incapable of rising above himself,
And traditional values winning out
Over an attempted independence of mind?
Second-lieutenant George Sherston went on strike against
                                    the war.
But his pacifism led him, not before a court-martial,
But into a hospital for the 'shell-shocked'.
There a psychiatrist, as clever as calm,
Coupled with plenty of good food and golf,
Restores Sherston to sanity.
He decided finally to return to the front,
Did so, found the job not too awfully awful don't you know,
Was wounded, and ended up
In a rather nobler type of hospital

[1] This poem, and the next, while not included in *The Battle Continues*, MacDiarmid's
Spanish War poem, were written at the same time and deal with the English reaction
to Spain and to war in general.

Where members of the royal family stopped by his bed
To offer forty-five seconds of polite sympathy,
And there the narrative ends, with Sherston as muddled
                                    as ever,
And given to rather vague – and glib – interrogations
That may be taken to express
His partial dissatisfaction with the universe.

As a transcript of a young man's actual emotions in war
The book is convincing enough. You must, however, regard
The young man as extremely average,
With no real self-knowledge
And no fixed scale of values.
He is anybody who has seen the blood and horror of war
Which is a great deal less than we are supposed
To take Sherston to have been. Furthermore,
Seeing that almost twenty years lie
Between Sherston's experiences
And the writing of them down
One looks for a sense of perspective,
A revision of values, a growth of understanding,
One nowhere encounters.
This is what happened to Sherston
And so far as the book is concerned
Nothing ever happened afterwards.

There is possibly an argument in favour
Of presenting things simply as they were,
Of leaving them inclosed
Within their own time and place,
Without hindsight, without revaluation;
Though it is not easy to put it forward here,
Since the Sherston of today constantly and pointedly
Keeps interjecting himself into the picture.
But what is really wrong with the book
Is the portrait of Sherston as he then was:

A man so quickly able to accommodate himself,
After one flare of defiance,
To prevailing sentiment.
It is not that Sherston was either
A weak or a cowardly person.
It is rather that his rebelliousness was only
Superimposed on his profoundly English nature.
It would be unfair to say that, after coming out
Against war and all it signified
He traduced his principles. Rather he changed his mind,
Regained the national disease of 'seeing things through',
Saw them through, and, ended up, pleased
That the royal family should stand by his hospital bed
And confer its verbal largesse. In other words
Sherston rebelled under stress of feeling
Then conformed again under stress of feeling;
Throughout the ordeal he was altogether
The victim of his emotions.

This is not the stuff the members
Of the International Brigade were made of.
This is not enough to create for me,
A provocative book.
Set against any of the better narratives of the war
By Continental writers, *Sherston's Progress* seems
Not only confused, but confused
In an immature and childish way.
In Mr Sassoon's book there is simply no evidence
Of a thinking mind; there is neither
Psychological nor philosophical substance.
There is only a young man who lets himself in
For a bad quarter of an hour, and then,
Not because he lacks courage,
But because he lacks conviction,
Falls back into the ranks.
His real interests are golf,

Chasing the fox, reading poetry;
Is it too cynical to think at times
That his real objection to the war
Is its interfering with these pleasures?

England's Double Knavery

The recent political turn of the people
Against ramps, impudence, lies, intrigues, and banditry
Proves, however, the antique dictum:
Never has a whole nation been seen to act wickedly.
Perhaps the literary world will turn next!
... But people do not like to be freed of a clog.
Sentimental and intellectual,
And I am ready to hear the barbarous noise
(Preluded in Roy Campbell's poem,[1] Garvin's writings
                                        and elsewhere)
Of Milton's pack of 'owls, cuckoos, asses, apes and dogs',
There will also be some grieved sighs,
And, I hope, some honourable amends.
But already every writer of any account is on our side;
Only Campbell, de Montalk,[2] and a few others,
Negligible scribblers, have gone the other way.
But with John Bull, the enemy of enemies,
The perfidy goes to infinitely greater depths
And passes through allotropic stages
Taking forms ill to connect with the first.
Among the unintelligent, who desire someone's disappearance,
Simple satisfaction of spite and rage is enough.
But no *plotter* ever yet aimed
At the mere downfall of his victim.
Although spite is ever the heating passion,
With Codlin as with Pecksniff, with Iago and all
There is always a cold passion down below.
Codlin wreaked his spite on Short as the real,
Though invisible, showman, but when he whispered
That Codlin was the Friend, not Short,

---

[1] 'Flowering Rifle' by the late Roy Campbell.
[2] Count Geoffrey Potocki de Montalk, Editor of *The Right Review*.

He heard the coins already rattling in his pocket
And saw himself honoured at the feast
And Short out in the cold.
Pecksniff not only manœuvred *de bon cœur*
To embroil the young Chuzzlewit with his friends;
He also stole the credit
For the design of the grammar-school.
Iago plotted
'To get his place and to plume up my will
In double knavery.'
This double knavery works so smoothly
It is hard to detect which half works first,
But it is certain that a cold passion lives with a man
And enters into *all* his behaviour,
Whereas spite needs special circumstances to make it
                                                    active,

This double knavery is so difficult to unmask
That dramatists and novelists are mostly driven
To call in coincidence and confession
To make a fair-play ending.
The victim is rarely in any sort of position
To defend himself, since only the unsuspecting
Can be victimised, and be his own character good,
Or even middling, and his brain a busy one,
Warning will fly past him,
So history of successful and glorified plotters.
There was only a stage-play slip
Between the cup and the lip of Iago
And, if he had *succeeded*, he would have heard
As many *Evvivas* as Mussolini
While forgotten Othello rotted in the earth,
And Cassio cooled his exiled heels in some Libya.
Hitler's June 30th hand finds many of the world's high folk
Willing to shake it.
But for the gift of the gab, neither Hitler nor Mussolini
Might ever have attracted any attention.

In England, though aspiring leaders still need to
                                     collect their crowd
By offering honey (with, of course, opportune threats
                                     of vinegar)
Inconvenient colleagues can be put out of the way
By that most discreet of poisons, the boycott.
(They do these things better in France . . . when a
                                     well-known officer tried
To organise a campaign of boycott
Against his former *amie* and colleague
Paris laughed – and someone crushed
The business with untranslatable wit:
'Mais ce coquin érige en juge litteraire
Son lingam dépite!'
But, also, the woman was on the spot,
Knew all the ropes, and fought like a lioness.)

It is very simple; you just say nothing.
The method is not vulgarly to bleed your victim
But to dry up his blood
(Though England prefers victims who begin by being restive,
They taste better afterwards – like birds
Cooked while their blood is still warm.)
England, every now and again, achieving
A larger subjugation of truth than ever before,
And delighted with the cleverness of her Cabinet ministers
When they show themselves most cynically dishonest,
Openly betraying all they simultaneously profess,
Building up incredible lies into self-congratulatory virtues!
England! – Can we cut out of our hearts that absurd old loyalty,
That half-shamed admiration which makes us feel
How clever it is of her always to be able
To get away from the disaster? She is so unscrupulous,
So selfish, so wilful, and so arrogant – and yet
Somehow or other she never has to pay for it.
But she is going to have to pay for it now

At compound interest, and to the uttermost farthing!
Most of the great social forces in the world today
Are like some quiet woman all her neighbours respect
And can imagine no ill of – yet she holds
Her husband under with hellish cruelty,
And may well drive her long-suffering family
To murder her at last. Well, murder's murder,
And society exacts the penalty, of course,
But let one of the family cry 'she deserved it'
And instantly the neighbours will denounce
The vilifier of the innocent dead (as they deem)
And defender of murder (no deed less deserved).
The family must suffer in silence to the end
And preserve the decent fiction, generally believed,
Obloquy and ostracism their portion if they don't.
– This is the age-long tyranny Campbell supports
(Royalty, Religion, and all the other quiet old women
Hocussing humanity with their old wives' tales,
And hiding infernal cruelty behind their quiet looks,
The remnants of the ancient Matriarchal system
That delayed the coming of civilisation for thousands of years
And still poisons it through and through!)
And conjures up in defence a fantastic picture
Of left-wing politicians stampeding with ill-got gold!
How much of the stolen wealth of the workers
Has ever found its way into left-wing pockets?
What tiny percentage of the bloody horror of war
Has ever been caused by the left? Every word of his poem
Has twenty tons of beef or mutton behind it,
He says – He is wrong.[1] The dead weight is neither
                                          beef nor mutton
But pork – sheer swinishness! And the several thousand
                                          tons of wheat
Is wrong too. The backing is nothing but hay-wire.

[1] Vide Roy Campbell's letter in *The Times Literary Supplement* of 25 February 1939.

Left-wing poetry represents a rise in the price of bread,
And starving workless peasants, a bread queue, a stricken field.
Represents is right, i.e. *Protests against!* – not *causes.*
That is the proud prerogative of Right-wing poetry
And since in Britain and America at least
The latter outbulks the former by ninety-nine to one,
Surely it could nullify the one per cent,
If there were any truth in the ludicrous charge?
How does Campbell explain its impotence?
His logic is as rotten as his poetry
And all his precious harvest can possibly produce
Is an epidemic of pellagra – the true
Harvest of the Right in very fact. Poor opisthocoelian
                                             Campbell,
The hollowest of all the hollow men, and so
Fit champion of his wholly indefensible cause,
Which, if it had been good, his bonehead gaucherie
Would have let down and ruined in any case!
Not that his typical reader would have known!
– A stout man, walking with a waddle, with a face
Creased and puffed into a score
Of unhealthy rolls and crevices
And a red and bulbous nose;
A rich man who fawns his way through life,
With a thick husky voice, naturally coarse,
Through which with grotesque insistence runs a tone
Of mock culture – a man whose fat finger
Ticks off the feet in Campbell's lines
'Left, right! Left, right!' and whose aesthetic sense
Delights to hear the recurrent crack
Of the hippopotamus hide whip or to note
The sibilance as of rubber truncheons every here and there.
So you went for a soldier, did you,
Campbell? – a soldier in Spain?
The hero of a penny novelette
With the brain of a boy scout!

All soldiers are fools.
That's why they kill each other.
The deterioration of life under the régime
Of the soldier is a commonplace; physical power
Is a rough substitute for patience and intelligence
And co-operative effort in the governance of man;
Used as a normal accompaniment of action
Instead of a last resort it is a sign
Of extreme social weakness. Killing
Is the ultimate simplification of life. And while
The effort of culture is towards greater differentiation
Of perceptions and desires and values and ends,
Holding them from moment to moment
In a perpetually changing but stable equilibrium
The animus of war is to enforce uniformity
– To extirpate whatever the soldier
Can neither understand nor utilise.